MONSTERS I HAVE BEEN

MONSTERS

I HAVE

BEEN

モンスターズになっていた俺

KENJI C. LIU

ALICE JAMES BOOKS
FARMINGTON, MAINE
ALICEJAMESBOOKS.ORG

10 9 8 7 6 5 4 3 2 1

Alice James Books are published by Alice James Poetry Cooperative, Inc., an affiliate of the University of Maine at Farmington.

Alice James Books
114 Prescott Street
Farmington, ME 04938
www.alicejamesbooks.org

Library of Congress Cataloging-in-Publication Data

Names: Liu, Kenji C., author.
Title: Monsters I have been / Kenji C. Liu.
Description: Farmington, Maine : Alice James Books, [2019] | Includes
   bibliographical references.
Identifiers: LCCN 2018038107 (print) | LCCN 2018040543 (ebook) | ISBN
   9781948579544 (eBook) | ISBN 9781938584985 (pbk. : alk. paper)
Classification: LCC PS3612.I928 (ebook) | LCC PS3612.I928 A6 2019 (print) |
   DDC 811/.6--dc23
LC record available at https://lccn.loc.gov/2018038107

Alice James Books gratefully acknowledges support from individual donors, private foundations, the University of Maine at Farmington, the National Endowment for the Arts, and the Amazon Literary Partnership.

ART WORKS.
arts.gov

amazon literary
partnership

Cover art: Tomokazu Matsuyama

CONTENTS

ACKNOWLEDGMENTS

Earlier, sometimes unrecognizable versions of poems in this manuscript appeared in various places, to which much gratitude is owed:

"Descending, throttle early, savagely," "Letter to Chow Mo-wan," and "Empire strikes" in *Anomaly*

"Maggie and Tony" and "Now I know what it's like" in *Apogee*

"Ritual against toxic masculinity" in *Arc Poetry Magazine*

"Drowsiness through my kiss" in *Discover Nikkei*

"Ultraman's lament for Shin Hayata, Year 1 / 1年" in *Dusie 19*

"Notorious rain" in *Gulf Coast*

"Dear Stranger" and "Visa" in *Poetry Northwest*

"Portrait of grandfather as a cowboy," "What I like about you 1," and "Gyoshoku danshi" in *Tongue Journal*

"The monstrosity: Notes towards a frankenpo" in the anthology *Of Color: Poets' Ways of Making*, edited by Amanda Galvan Huynh & Luisa A. Igloria (The Operating System, 2019)

"Manifest destiny for sassy choir" in the anthology *Only Light Can Do That: 100 Post-Election Poems, Stories, and Essays* (The Rattling Wall and PEN Center USA, 2017)

The process of this book has relied on mutual exchange and the intellectual-emotional labor of many, both living and not. For me to write gender calls for situating myself in several lineages: The women of my family—Hori, Tani, Ishizaka, Liu, Lin, Peng, and Weng—whose daily labors continue to cascade through my generation. My intellectual and spiritual lineage, which forms the how and why of poetics for this book—especially Homi Bhabha, Judith Butler, Theresa Hak Kyung Cha, and Theravada Buddhism. My chosen family—beloved writing conspirator and union comrade Vickie Vértiz, with whom all things are possible. Hari Alluri, Kazumi Chin, Dan Lau, Muriel Leung, Barbara Jane Reyes, Margaret Rhee, Heidi Andrea Restrepo Rhodes, and the SGV Food Club for inspiring, encouraging, cajoling, and challenging. Cathy Linh Che and all the fellows, staff, and faculty of Kundiman—who gave parts of this book a place to think and breathe.

A special thanks to Carey Salerno and everyone at Alice James for believing in this book.

This work is in no way meant to encompass the totality of variations of gender or masculinity that are possible to express. May we tear down the conditions that allow the enclosure, commodification, exploitation, and marginalization of life's wondrous variety. Numberless beings, may we all be free.

FRANKENPO

[**frang**-kuh n-poh]

NOUN
1. an invented poetic form

VERB
2. to create a new poetic text by collecting, disaggregating, randomizing, rearranging, recombining, erasing, and reanimating one or more chosen bodies of text, for the purpose of divining or revealing new meanings often at odds with the original texts.

VISA

frankenpo

1.

Dear love,
I have arrived in
the national hair.

Already, my prey nerves
are in the burn of growth
the ongoing build
of god
mucus.
Everywhere, government
sponsored fanaticism
multiple acts of teeth.
Our love in a time
of inappropriations
of malicious inadmissibility.
The under
state
swarms our
documents. Our
lungs.

2.

Dear proclamation,

how many

statutory galaxies in

a single body? My internal

shape

hemmed in

by procedural pleura. I am

a subsection

of light

drowning

in a fiscal country, where

case by case   life

remains

in the shape

of prayer.

Dear disaster,

today I was

a swarm border

a spleen of

biometric information

pliable synovial data.

I was day

light

in an embassy

of flesh.

In bones, fat

the gift immigrants

of us

water asks for

reciprocity.

Here we rain

everything.

4.

Thus have I heard:

We are visas

        in a national

        drowning.

        Each of us an executive

    decision, pursuant to clay.

Each a subsection

    of protocol

        and yet.

    Memoranda: I am a train light

      country

vetting

the president of

    his

    terrorist

    shape.

PORTRAIT OF GRANDFATHER AS A COWBOY

Western Village (ウエスタン村) *haikyo, Tochigi, Japan*

You aim

    at the national sky,[空]

say

    you don't suffer.[被らない]
    Beyond ripe,
        you puff away
        days
in a saloon,
    seated before

a persimmon.[熟柿]

        Summer. We fly[飛ばせられる]

    thousands[千千]

    of miles[マイルス]
        to be
        your cigarette.
    Your six-
cylinder heart
blows
    and blasts,
        eyes and neck
    a-stutter,

    a moon-[月]

    crazed owl.[気が変]

Drawl

    in lazy Japanese—

          Charles
          チャールズ,

             Elvis
             エルヴィス,

           Clinton
           クリント,

       Marilyn
       マリリン.

    Littering the air
with carbon
and menthol
    flitter.
       The animatronic

     国旗   栄誉礼
     flag. Salute!

    アメリカの
    America's

  亡霊
ghost
in your

     露
    exposed
      hydraulics,
      and fields
of rock-
headed
    presidents.

      共和国
     A republic

     下
  of bees under

  頭皮
the scalp.

ULTRAMAN'S LAMENT FOR SHIN HAYATA, YEAR 1 / 1年

1. In this memory you're a cold rattle of pills. A pressed gathering of molecules, rejected by gravity.

2. In Nagasaki, the holes were the deepest in the world. They weren't that deep. It's not what you wanted, was it.

3. You're an aluminum horse slipping between the snowflakes, your ragged split of hair whistling waist-long. Now a view of the asylum's burned caramel.

4. If you're looking, you should fall into a sinkhole in the tundra. Giant flocks of birds will pass over. Deep, not a measurement, just a statement of fact.

5. What did it take to carve your lovely nose? Slip through the crabgrass kingdom with that glass ballerina spine. A reputable spectre always returns to hunger.

6. That winter, the first time a diagnosis ever touched you. No testosterone in the tank. How many times has a fist of hail found your exact location?

7. You haven't been as sad as the gazing moon. But you've lived in a suburb. What's the only medicine that's ever worked for you?

8. Sketch your name in your palm. Count the strokes. How many now? The blue orb of your Ultraman, draining like a god ventricle. The unusual ruin of your manliness. 男らしいの荒廃

9. A crater in the shape of you and nothing to fill it with. Isn't that enough? Crash down to me, become ice.

WHAT I LIKE ABOUT YOU 1

after Kenneth Tam's "Breakfast in Bed"

Bro, you're lanky and tall. Your eyes really stand out.

Got a lot of hair growing from your chest, spilling.

I'm jealous of your beard, it's nice and full. Jealous.

You look like you take care of yourself. When we dance,

I love the way our bells swing. Got a good physique,

you're a good-looking guy. We coordinate well.

You've got good ideas, like swinging our hips right

and then left. You take leadership, appreciate that.

I chase you with blue paint and you spring away.

I want to make my mark on you, like all the other guys.

Love your skin tone, darker than mine. Let me glue

this cheerio to your chest. I'll avoid the hair. Though dusky,

your skin's bright under fluorescents. This blindfold fits

perfectly under your tinfoil hat. Find me, bro.

I'm rustling in the far corner. I'm circling, watching, and

smiling. I'm teasing your neck. Let's hold hands and jingle.

TEACHING MEN TO BE EMOTIONALLY HONEST

frankenpo

My full teeth desire was
to avoid being[1]

an extracurricular
victim[2]

of minor men
in the ugly experiment[3]

The tough-guy lines
suicide hookups[4]

pounding displays of
national gender[5]

---

1. An inheritance of undershirts. This extra lady hotline. A reputation for independent he-love, distracted beer sensibilities, money toilets, and tone attack captains.

2. "When I was a very small boy / very small boys talked to me / now that we've grown up together / they're afraid of what they see"

3. Otherwise known in certain circles as an "I statement." But instead, he saw through a 35 mm lens at all times.

4. You boxes are truly men inside. It's a lovely master destiny, society's carving points growing a thing.

5. "Hateful things: a man who has nothing in particular to recommend him discusses all sorts of subjects at random as though he knew everything."

These gesture projects
with their pall
facial crises[6]

    The stirring said: Be joy
    Mutate the hypermasculine
    kit[7]

Lower the
outpouring bicep and
devastating bark[8]

In that last behavior
point   a space of concision
gritted eye analysis[9]

What masks
What power[10]

---

6. "… a pervasive cluster of forces ranging from physical brutality to control of consciousness, which suggests that an enormous potential counterforce is having to be restrained."

7. For every himself, call it a bottom-feeder. "For the suit men of power." We turn among ourselves. The traditional boss ladder excuse, the cocktail I-am-so-manly-I-don't-care glances club, that no-brainer hell circle.

8. See Chinese Exclusion Act of 1882 and Page Act of 1875.

9. "I don't need your help. I just need you to recognize that this shit is killing you, too, however much more softly, you stupid motherfucker, you know?"

10. You poor expectation. You thing-master you.

to grow against this
hosted masculinity[11]

to rename by changing
a behavioral gap[12]

To be a thing of new gravity
in the tenuous
intimacy theater[13]

---

11. He was never told how to act, but he was measured in other ways.

12. "Están ahí, sí. Pero no existen."

13. "Whatever living beings there may be, whether they are weak or strong, omitting none. Outward and unbounded, freed from hatred and ill-will" (translated in forthcoming editions as "emotional labor").

GYOSHOKU DANSHI

魚　　Here's a fish with salt
食　　on his shoulder
男
子　　　　the ocean's best
　　　tasting son. His meat
　　　a test of stamina

in a city ceramic.

Overshadowed
by glowing Fukushima
plumes. Waiting

    for low tide with
a bloated moon
on his back.

I've been grilled
over my own
    sadness.

I've been
my own patch
of drought grass

    seams split by
someone else's
heat.

The serrated edge
of patience
and my belly its
nest.

After this, I have no guts
to tie, no sausage joy.

I'll drive your bus
into the barbeque
        pit and burn clean
through the bones

        your true-blue
dinosaur charcoal.

Wrap yourself in sugar
barnacles.

        You're encrusted with tacks.
With snacks.

I'm here to write
a different man.

Shouldn't we taste like
        warm, milky milk?

Drift into me
        fish. I'm the sweetest
seawccd you'll ever

lick. Your devoted
        brackish coil of stars.

Your boss radio signal
aimed

        galactic north.

RAJESH GOES TO THE STUD CLUB

after Qurbani (1980)

O, lonely heart
without love you will suffer

It's a dark forest beneath
our open polyester shirts

In the meager air between us
chest hair weaves a bridge

O, may your heavy gold chains
hang low just for me

We're two cocky
simple-celled organisms

Your chin wags lucky
You're a gangster for me

You make my jiggly show
glow incandescent

Behind this extra sideburn
a burning pink rose

My tears in your ascot
now salty jewels, you slip away

After we dance, tell me
where you'll bury your thieving fists

It will be great
Yes, yes life will be great

Someone like you
should come into my life

Before they lock you up
let's rumble and roll around

Love, jump on my
magnificent haystack

Our Superman hearts
disco-ing out of control

I'll wiggle my flower
so your eyebrow will rise

You could be smashing
my Mercedes
with your mustache

You could be proposing
to my biceps in a canary
rubber dinghy

It will be great
Yes, yes life will be great

After we dance, caress me
with your nightstick

Flip me, toss me
Smother me with bell-bottoms

I can't quit the way you
defenestrate my affection

Love, keep direct eye contact
with my smirky turtleneck

I'm not an angel
just a half-smoked cigarette

RAJESH'S THEME

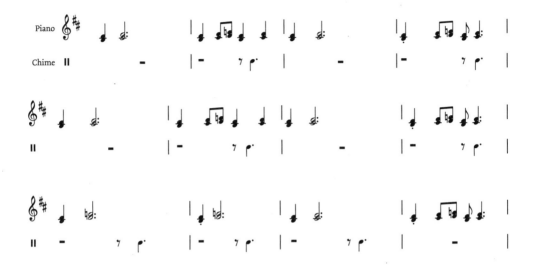

SELF-PORTRAIT AS HIKARU, SHINING LIGHT

after Star Trek, *"The Naked Time" (1966) S1:E4*

1.

Hands raised in praises
of an orange night,

Hikaru meets the color of things
in a nightclub. He's dust

ripples, a smash of tangerine
on the walls,

a pair of weaving beacons
for hands.

Hikaru—warm, mineral
cloud of smoke.

—no, a midnight wet
with warehouses

and a powdery melon moon
for an eye. No

a hatchbacked boy looking
for a kiss.

2.

Yes, a flash of gangly elbows and
slick sweat chest,

a skinny stack of pretty boy
driving up all starry turnpikes.

Hallway: a young man offers
his lips and Hikaru pours his peaches in.

Light is the taste of
salt and cream. A naked time.

Portrait as phosphorescent
wriggle in wide-legged pants.

If Light had a prism, he'd drop
a glitter bomb on this weekend.

3.

The ocean might choke your
new copper penny tomorrow.

Your fair maiden or man
might be neither. Whose skin

will you touch when you want
to touch Light? Whose navel

is the honest home, where you
can be a pair of shiny lips—and

not a wrong
-pointed rapier in the dusk?

FOOTNOTES TO A MURDER IN THE THIRD DEGREE

frankenpo for Michael Chun Hsien Deng

after Jenny Boully

---

1. You are our glass of anxiety. Our night cravings slam you into a terrible dream American.

2. Yes the clutching, roughly bent shove. We mount our history, groaning, misshapen. We pull flowers, console each other's dusky daggers. We broken brothers, tackling each other with belonging.

3. Tackling: "... to physically interfere with the forward progress of a player... such that his forward progress ceases and is not resumed..."

---

4. I too am a blundering translation. A red, beaten trophy.

5. While viewing Justin Lin's film *Better Luck Tomorrow*, the author left the theatre at this point.

6. If spirit ever comes beautiful, it is occupied country. Supplanted and blurry. A desperate kettle.

7. "The Duke said, 'Excellent! Indeed, if the ruler is not a ruler, the ministers not ministers, fathers not fathers and sons not sons, even if I have food, how can I eat it?'"

8. During this performance, slow rotation from stage left to right. Four iterations: child, peacock, hammer, capture.

9. "Her son was already past saving, but she decided to keep him breathing so that his father would have time to arrive from China. That night, she stayed by Michael's bedside and stuck acupuncture needles in his arm in a desperate attempt to save her son."

10. Your death suit fits ornately on my back.

11. Burning heaven bank notes in an empty field in the Poconos, note direction of the floating ashes. Photo credit: the author.

12. "To extract each fragment by each fragment from the word from the image another word another image the reply that will not repeat history in oblivion."

_____

13. I am a furnished move, imprecise, a sprawling.

14. "The modern Asian American fraternity was born out of the protests of the '80s and the growing alienation that Asian Americans felt on campus."

15. Our enclaves of handsome shoulders, islands of palanquin anxiety. High-functioning immigrants making churches of hoodies.

16. "… 'male bonding,' which may, as in our society, be characterized by intense homophobia, fear, and hatred of homosexuality."

17. Illegible, possibly an asemic strategy: "Asian American scholarship and activism... whose urgency has been hollowed out by years of apathy..."

18. "How does it feel / when you treat me like you do / and you've laid your hands upon me / and told me who you are"

19. A fluttering, untranslatable concept.

20. Grave sweeping, a flower of rituals similar to Hexagram 23, splitting apart. "Your swollen, trembled halt. To us, deeply acceptable."

SHE'S PEOPLE! 10 APOLOGIES

frankenpo

1. I came of age in a national innocent man, I.

2. Now, I don't believe these events. Understand, I am a man wracked with grace.

3. I gladly listen, uncomfortable, but I.

4. I offended women, but I'm founded in great hardship. I has stories, hope, grace, touching excuses, I.

5. This is my regret basket. Honestly, I'm the last accountable man, think I.

6. Beyond victims, my wake-up record is clear. A depth of career party consciousness. A gubernatorial man pursuing hotly.

7. Spiritual intentions. Ethics, coincidental.

8. You believe the attacks and predicament videos? Non-consensual but good-natured.

9. My behavior cannot have been seriously, sincerely remiss, a double-digit nothing. I deserve a superhero investigation.

10. It's not an excuse. Time will apologize.

DEAR I CHING, AM I A REAL MAN?

ほんとのおとこはなにですか

Nourish the prince, and heaven becomes
a fixed space—a head of danger.

A system of melancholy, this man paradise.
An inward mass of ambush.

Your antithesis heart.
You are quarrelsome water, upward rain.

The preceding image: a difficult bridge,
an entangled chariot of imperial muscle.

A disorder declining towards the animal.
A stringman, drawn away, receding.

Time is superior in its direction,
but even among the dead, atoms conflict.

See this cloud, pervasive,
borderless.

Do not ask again.

Deep earlight, you could be fuel for gender thievery.
A majestic encroachment.

STOMACH ME, DELICIOUS WORLD

frankenpo

Hong Kong—

Their government ugly makes our colony drunk.
It's a fuckwad Victorian-era fight. The slaughterhouse follows us,
sleep-eating. Asking for más meat.

This happy visiting hole.

And my soap voice husband. Turning over, he says—in immaculate parentheses—
we deserve beautiful between wars. A love body, a dumpling. At least
a lovely face, some pretty piedra enclosed in jungle. For my sticky birthday
let's go unfilial. Go national shit line.

I've been needed in English—
a small, hard voice pawing my night.

This is invocation. Or divination. We're bruises, an unconstitutional ceremony
of dirt. We won't feel the dead come. We're brighter
birds, cucurrucucú. No llores, our messed flesh sleep,
        and what was I,
                apart from your law.

MAGGIE AND TONY

frankenpo

This birthday detrimental, let's eat undesirable men,
rice congee, Taiwan Beer, lick emasculated stitches.

No, let's eat spectrum definitions, hypermasculine
pork, average noodles, drunk business men.

Let's eat asleep men craving toxic enjoyable, with a taste for
submissive sesame, standing sex, cautious sticky vegetable.

Fussy steam lunch. More fluid nonbinary men please, some halfway
polite, rice cake anomaly serving mah jong noodles al dente.

Dinner walks in the rain! Creep scene with angry soup fish. Hungry
dead in the unpacking mirror. Empty shoes.

Tonight, who will dismantle? Strange, virile men in a tea lunch
typhoon? Who wants the beautiful hole of deprived objects?

HELLO STRANGER

after the film Moonlight

I was a child gripped by the sand
at the bottom of your sea.

I was not a loud thing, though
my eyes thieved across your chin.

That rise, the moon shook my tongue.
In the wet gulf between us, our skin blue.

Ooo, seems like a mighty long time.
For ten years I've been that night.

Become a thicket of muscle
and gold-lined cracks.

A body that rattles and hisses,
even during the quiet of sleep.

Not a lamb, but a blood fight.
Our black was thick with teeth.

I only know what I barely knew
and none of it could be said.

The moon, an underwater beast
pressing me to spill.

Haven't we slapped the hips of this song before?
I'm taller than any man's knuckles. Even yours.

I am the slow burn. *Who is you.*
You emptied my life, and I jumped through.

WE LEARN TO BE MEN

Wind shaped like a boy comes
riding
a leather-headed spit[1]

Twirling up a new country from the corn
his rifle deep kisses first necks until
they vanish from the books[2]

By what device and special
button combo is civility   burned to bacon[3]

Meat the hidden code
an ode to any president[4]

---

1. A bird or a free thing, ridden through by a flame.

2. Of the painting, Crofutt wrote: "A diaphanously and precariously clad America floats
   westward thru the air with the 'star of empire' on her forehead. She has left the cities of the
   east behind, and the wide Mississippi, and still her course is westward. In her right hand she
   carries a school book—testimonial of the national enlightenment, while with her left she
   trails the slender wires of the telegraph that will bind the nation. Fleeing her approach are
   Indians, buffalo, wild horses, bears, and other game, disappearing into the storm and waves of
   the Pacific coast. They flee the wondrous vision—the star 'is too much for them.'"

3. A teetering distaste, drunk gravity: "Not welded together by gold but bound."

4. スヘール　ハマッド:「あなたが叩いている肌を親密に知っている。」
   Suheir Hammad: "I know / intimately that skin / you are hitting."

Windy boy knows where the whip lands
it always carves a manly name[5]

To have nothing but a tiny bird to wrap
a fist around[6]

Its compressed flight a commentary

We are each a world and its daily dying[7]

An aviary turned inside
out and tightened[8]

---

5. Yet how the warp spreads. Its head crackles into space, attempts to bridge away from the burn.

6. "A ceramic shoe for the king," here a clay fist pushes outward into vacuum. All the inner steam was scared cold.

7. Shōbijin: "Mothra oh Mothra / if we were to call for help / over time, over sea, like a wave / you'd come / our guardian angel"

8. Without epoxy, how can this man be an uncracked egg?

WHAT I LIKE ABOUT YOU 2

after Kenneth Tam's "Breakfast in Bed"

I've been noticing you. Got a great physique.

Your hair's awesome, nice and long, beard's nice and full.

Straight up top and below all rough. You're pretty

hairy. That's good, means you got a lot of testosterone.

It's a good sign. You're relaxed, even when I'm trying

to finger you with paint. You keep jumping away.

I shake my tinfoil horns, try to draw you closer.

Gentle you behind the ear. Swing my bells at you.

Lie down with your shirt off? Talk to me about

your girl. I'll paste cheerios around your nipples like

the other guys. Maybe you'll get married. I like your skin

complexion, you know, just a good tone, good skin.

No one here but us, shirtless. No windows, just beers

and a closed door. I'm here with you to be a man.

DEAR I CHING, WHAT IS THE LEGACY OF COLONIZATION IN MY FAMILY?

か	At the arcade
ら	the co-prosperity sphere lines up
だ	quarters and
が	
○	this is how it all starts
○	
○	to disintegrate

~

Customs did not check my luggage. After I left the gate, I saw they were waiting to welcome us. I had not seen this daughter for a long time.

Shōryūken!
Hadouken!

昇　波
龍　動
拳　拳
！　！

We took the electric train to Osaka City. Those lights flashed in the dark like colorful flowers. It made the night even more beautiful.

Thunder bursts through
the sleepy ground

Uniformed partisans
mount the splendid bloom

    hit down, down, down, up

    ~

I stayed at home, meditated, and read Buddhist sutras. He saw me doing this and he explained it was because of electric waves in the air, so not to be afraid.

We tiny emperors
unlock levels, obey the convulsion

Our hot burrs spread
one hundred thousand miles

~

The sky should have been darker since it was evening, however when I looked down from the flight, I could see a lot of red and green lights.

Multiplication
the supreme calculation
of thirst

~

Today I woke up earlier than before. There were doves in the yard flying here and there, not afraid of people. We took a picture together.

o
rolling thunder

afflict a new beginning

ドカーン！！！

The sunshine came out. It was very beautiful.

Shock began
prosperity will end

Our uranium bruises

Scent of corrupt pineapple

~

What I felt cannot be described by pen.

Soured fluids
pour out

in libation.

Adjusted my spirit and raised my qi. You only need to turn a corner to get there.

NOTORIOUS RAIN

frankenpo: Mifune Toshiro in Manchukuo

Why weren't we told the rain
would trample our darkening fields?

To the disaster, there's only
wind to testify.

How do the dead say, *This ruined temple
is my body?*

Their docile leathers are
drunk with the eyes of insects.

In the vested woods
one of us is horse,

a war heart crossing the midst.
An espionage.

Is August not a famine, December not a rope?
わしが。。。わしの心が分からない。
(*I...I don't understand my own soul.*)

And upstream, our national defense—
a crying kimono with eight eyes, a six-faced priest.

Why does the secretary of bodies
authorize such lavish feathers?

分かんない。さっぱり分かんない。
(*I don't understand. I just don't understand.*)
We crouch with terrible faith. An enemy beautiful.

ULTRAMAN'S LAMENT FOR SHIN HAYATA, YEAR 5 / 5年

Memory, you're cold. A pressed gathering, a gravity. In Nagasaki, the tiger slips between ash flakes. The red hole. Pass over measurement and facts and carve your lovely nose, your glass spine. With a reputable hunger. The first time a diagnosis ever touched your exact location. You haven't been the moon. The only medicine, your name. How many now? The ruin of you and nothing. Isn't that enough?

Memory, a pressed gravity. The hole, a measurement. Facts: your lovely glass spine, a reputable hunger. The first diagnosis? Exact location: the moon. Your name, how many? The ruin that isn't enough.

Memory, the hole. Glass hunger. Diagnosis: the moon. How many ruins?

The hole. Hunger. The moon.

I BITE WITH INACCURATE TEETH

frankenpo

Dear love,

a life of good conduct and   a festering depression under.   pus nationalists cling to

the spleen well. this dissolving   unadaptable country—how   the white charnel ground

offers its despoiled body.   rotten segments pass through   the official pleura.

an intestinal consciousness.   as always our bodies are   slaughters in the making

historical beings of nuclear bile   mesentery lamentation.   in the precious crush of national arousings

we become, again   weapons against the immigrated.   a haunting perception arisen we

long blue animals defiled by   an economy of suspicion.   instill the spectre of venereal

nationalism, as if objects of calming.   blood clings to the wastelands   skin on the election door.

The delusional state—shiny, shiny, shiny.

MANIFEST DESTINY FOR SASSY CHOIR

frankenpo

desolation its operations

futurity eternal

and and and salvation

we of proportionate liberties a death

-conscious organization set in what history

our mission of of of

our entirely destined ——

myriad greatness

democratic hierarchs

and the the the principles

derived of effulgence and cynosure

immutable everlasting

on to the retrograde

on National earth

the history of happiness

suffer glory

we freedom victims

patriots shall

the nation objects

supremacy to all all all

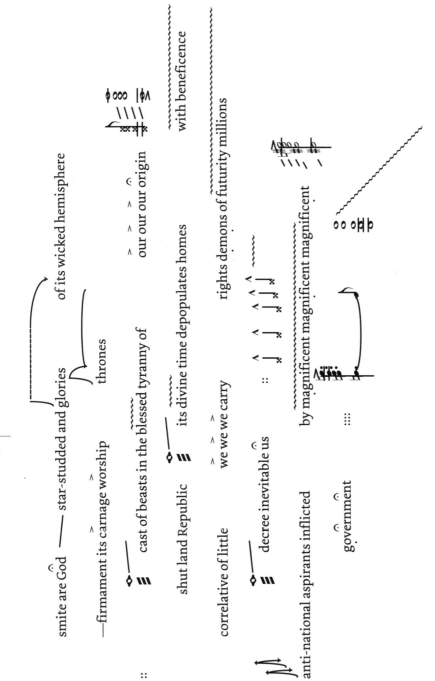

with beneficence

of its wicked hemisphere

our our our origin

rights demons of futurity millions

thrones

smite are God ——— star-studded and glories

—firmament its carnage worship

cast of beasts in the blessed tyranny of

its divine time depopulates homes

shut land Republic

we we we carry

correlative of little

decree inevitable us

by magnificent magnificent magnificent

anti-national aspirants inflicted

government

PORTRAIT OF GRANDFATHER AS A ROBOT COWBOY

You aim at the national sky,
in a saloon, seated before a persimmon.
We fly thousands of miles to be your cigarette,
eyes and neck a-stutter, moon-crazed owls.

In a saloon, seated before a persimmon—
チャールズ, エルヴィス, クリント, マリリン。
Eyes and neck a-stutter. A moon-crazed owl and
an animatronic flag. Salute!

チャールズ, エルヴィス, クリント, マリリン,
littering the air with menthol flitter.
An animatronic flag. Salute!
America's ghosts in their exposed hydraulics.

Littering the air with menthol flitter,
we fly thousands of miles to be your cigarette.
America's ghosts in your exposed hydraulics,
you take aim at the national sky.

NOW I KNOW WHAT IT'S LIKE

frankenpo

> *I knew now that I had to make another monster.*
> —Dr. Frankenstein

His interminable body harbored
hidden men—

bomb gallantries,
warfare cognates.

The crucial interior, numbed
to turn the curse of affect,

thought modification
with unending character
limits.

A vessel of spinning,
obliquely propelled man fears,

and want-passengers,
sad monsters of all broke states.

His compulsive
nation of narcissistic guns,

grief men, shooting
home.

Wars of syndicated motion threading across

a slowly enormous realm.

That night, I ran everyone wrong.

I told the monster that I would make
a wife for him.

Even with centuries of variant
hyper-genders,

a hundred gender chances,
I dreamed too ugly.

My man components loyal
to a freaked system of father loops.

Body threw all.

The lust economy
carcassing mercilessly.

This need for
mechanisms.

For national monster workshops
that shake graves.

When I made the first creature,
I didn't know how it would turn out.

A knowledge machine of silent
man children.

The dead gazing back,
and I, their creature.

DEAR I CHING, HOW DOES HETEROPATRIARCHY LIVE ON THROUGH ME?

(you/your)

劉さま　　　have no meaning yet.

The king arrives at noon.
His wife has been a fruitful
arm to rely on. Convenient.

Despite what　　劉さん　　have lost,
　　　　　　　　あなたさま　are called to get the benefit.
　　　　　　　　あなた　　　have money in
　　　　　　　　おたく　　　hometown.
　　　　　　　　きみ　　　　need to marry fertile soil.

Please try whether the solar eclipse.
　　In the thunder here, set　じぶん　　name, the growth of obligation.
All the lines are old, and hide
a lot of resources.

　　　　　　Do___change　あんた　　mind slowly? How rich it is.
　　　　　　　　　　　　おまえ　　face the order. It is not the truth.
　　　　　　　　　　　　こいつ　　feel conquered, a tragic sadness.
　　This great bubble is　きさま　　second hometown.
　　　　　　　　　　　　てめえ　　have provided the ritual part
　　　　　　　　　　　　　　　　　　of its acquisition. Which means
　　　　　　　　　　　　　　　　　　the end of the cost of living here.

　　We plan the future　おのれ　　belong to.
Your war does not deviate
from the war.

WANTED BODIES BECOME ANIMALS

frankenpo

Children of
cutting
bone mayhem,

BITTER
chemistry, and
no NATIONAL
smile—

Time dies
IN THE punch
OF **everything**.

In the
west, **how**

wanted bodies become
pretty
secrets, how
we become
animals.

How the NATION'S
ghost PROSTATE
jerks
cowboy-caliber men
into SHIVERED
war **rodeos**.

How WE man-
gather,
CIRCLING guns,
shaking,
SWALLOWING
hard
youngsters OF simple
murders, smile face
rifle hits,
GESTAPO FUCKING
in PRESCRIPTION costumes.

America animals.

Flash! See liquor
BODIES, ROTTEN
PUBIC worms, and WE
their BEASTS.

Tentacles
and the white
drizzle of sweat
ammo.

Holes
in every once-
animal.

EMPIRE STRIKES

frankenpo

Citizens of the civilized galaxy, on this day we mark a transition. Billions of helpless factors wind us into blinding, black-gloved sparks. The pain constantly beautiful, omnipotence ripped by a giant Jedi abyss. Great ears of the people stolen, deathly half governors, and bureaucracy, that unstoppable depletion. Nation of my gracious physiognomy, once we prospered entire, every fiction time! Our last infrastructure collapses black, we sink wicked, a feeble station, infused by a never-ending crawl. Our regions are semidarkness, with scarred and weak edges, groans along our peace borders, ripped, scattered, dimly white. Against the reaped verdict, storm troopers ignite, my dark hood star attacks, lord I. Your unbearable boy emperor—my force fictitious flashes out, unstoppable bleed. My carnage grown from exaggerated disrepair. Seven foot tall in the well of a mob. Towards a cold room, our body staggers.

DROWSINESS THROUGH MY KISS

frankenpo

Dear Beloved,

Ill will wants to hew
you into smoke

A country is
a husk deception
a demon bottle

a mad gizzard
(black and blue from gender)
coming to crash
your wild inside canvas

Up the forest lunges
moans a shaking beard
spits a body
of spreading trousers

See forever
that serpent you annoyed

You bull moon
You skull prince rolling
for miles
your back
a barbed anatomy

You
high-heeled express

in a pure-heart jacket
in satin boy kneecaps
and a skinny pink
unicorn suit

You powder all the pieces
unlace the prettiest voice-over
lipstick could ever kill

Lion ears, you know
the balcony crumbles behind
you

And still the moon
protrudes
above
a purring
one-eyed wonder

See
clumsy love still runs
something

DESCENDING, THROTTLE EARLY, SAVAGELY

frankenpo (for Prince)

He's a beautiful bird again. Desperately funk, tornado gorgeous, heart thick with furious glide, and me his dessert. A conspiring body of heavy love, a whole dusk package. He sits and moistens, a ripeness in him. Glisten he rises, a burning of bites and roses. A flushed, trembling hollow across his lush. See his national pouty-lip, a skintight, slightly welling back door swinging all piano wide. His bikini simmers, his cheeks jump, honey face staring wickedly over lustrous flower shoulder. He crushes my diamonds, stains my quiver on the spot. I muzzle his leopard face. The night furrows its savage, purple coat. Waters my sleeping moonlight Cadillac. Drowning looks like light, a meaningless swim. Here, lustrous racked chrome, passport of spandex lips. His pompadour bird, plunging into my wild Minnetonka.

LETTER TO CHOW MO-WAN

frankenpo

Dear Mr. Chow,

Cherished seed. A sesame kiss, and you mend the distance between us. That deep dissonance. When will our smoke overlap again なの? Together we are a pair of lonely questions, differentiated, two who whisper open a category. Plural, Argus-eyed. Divination is a meaningful mesh. We call us home, multi-capillaried. We promise a beautiful object. A rare orientation わね.

Unthreatened can still be afraid. No injury is respectful. *This is because the caress is not a simple stroking; it is a shaping.* I am obsessed with the feeling of a house on fire. Do you agree なの? I am never going to end in a field of reason. Truth cannot go in the gaps. We are fool things わよ, precisely alive, mountainous.

MY BOY BAND THROWS NATIONAL SHADE

Gather. Listen full. I'm the velvet crash of a grand piano. Pain-faced from losing you, you, you. [*pull back, wide-angle*] A lake, a big-mouthed country swimming with small sads.

[*jump cut*] I raise my right princess hand, punch my own damn pixel bricks. I'm bionic, a pure gift of chiseled   eyebrow   sovereignty.

The border identifies my plumage—hello ma'am. *Have you ever seen attack ships on fire off the shoulder of Orion?* Have you ever been unzipped by a dichotomy?

My dance crew's back from break. Aren't we your secret preference? Immigrants of glitter in a world violently civil.

Stay there, slick your feathers back.
Croon.

We have no choice. [*montage*] Bump uninvited extremists off the stage. Moisturize into a J-pop boy band. Ungrow the trick mustache.

Our smooth man cheeks, a threat to America. There is no place for us, except in life.
[*voice-over*] We molt, flap open. Sing the queen body.

We jump the hollow bones of a map we draw ourselves.

ULTRAMAN'S LAMENT FOR SHIN HAYATA, YEAR 10 / 10年

That winter was gray with bone ash

The oaks sank thick

No serotonin in the tank

Tiny black holes rattled the throat

胸につけてるマークは流星 | *The mark in his chest is a meteor*

In Nagasaki the crater

Punched without permission

Ash fell into the red-mapled street

Slipping between snowflakes, a tiger

From the bottom of your hole

A measurement that cannot escape

A spinning glass ballerina spine

And your lovely nose

光の国から僕らのために | *From the Land of Light for the sake of us*

Reputable national spectre, starving black hole

First time a diagnosis ever touched you

Your exact location and a fist of hail

The moon punched the night

Was that your only medicine

A blue orb draining like a god ventricle

百万遍ワットの輝きだ | *The radiance of a million watts*

Your name in my palm, how many strokes

The ruin of you

Shaped like an invitation

THE GOAT MAN CANCELS HIS ENEMIES

frankenpo

                A magic collector
in a night
        of enmity.
                A boy flashlight,
        an insidious
                        instrument
arrived in
        unhandsome
                        lands. We all were
blurred beings,
        breathing and
                leaking
        fraudulent
        sounds. As if
                        all limbs and
                spines. Our manhood
was imprisoned
        back
                in the sea. As a salted
                fish I
                        violated
        heaven,
a misdemeanor

to the nose.

        So many

colonizing winters,

    customhouse anxieties.

            The newspapers

      moaning

      constantly

in condemnation

            of our stars. Their gender vision

      upon our hordes,

our thousand

vessels.

Their golden

murders.

    I burned a prayer

downward

      until it became

  a location

        for my body. In a heaven shortage,

  we became

a system of

      praise. If human was

  a bullet,

we were the blessed

recapture

      of inhuman

      pleasure. We were

southern water birds

    strapped

      to thunderbolt

      medicine. Dragon

   bells.

A blessed cargo,

   crashing the sanctity

      of national

thirst.

SELF-PORTRAIT AS VOLTRON

Before I was a man, I was a cat. Asleep in a life. From a kitten galaxy, I fell. Through a dirty cake of clouds. Burned my way into the earth.

Bon, how pleasant bon is, those who have parted from us, come to meet openly with us
盆はな盆は嬉しや、別れた人も、晴れてこのよえ、会いに来る

Perhaps a reluctant sun decorated the sky. A sun, or a circle of fluorescent not yet warm from the switch. My head betrayed me. I began to play a soggy frosted flake.

The clouds, from between the clouds, an envious moon comes to see the dancing
雲のな雲の間から、羨ましげに、踊り見に来た、お月様

I hid a man in my chest. Buried even the shadow of his shadow. A lake for a nest, and I the submerged. So many cold-toe nights. If someone had told me muscle was simply protein, and my tail, a laser. An elemental whir, straining against habit.

The dance, if you dance the dance, clap your hands, we can't sing without a rhythm
踊りな踊り踊るなら、手びょし叩け、調子付けなきゃ、歌も出ぬ

If we could steer this invasion together, coordinate the invocation. *Activate interlocks. Dyna-therms connected.* We could leap through a fruity pebble donut, connect fang foot to ass. Close my mouth around a blazing sword, and finish the exhausted sentence.

This evening, this evening's moon just as it is, we imagine our ancestors enjoying the afterlife
居易な今宵出た月は、神輿の月よ、親の御所楽、見て暮らす

My neighborhood flips over onto its scar-faced back. How to put the senses back together, how to assemble the machinery of my house? I have so many side-eyes. I want to be the right man, but not just any.

Dance, to dance and chant the Nenbutsu, with ease of spirit you won't be unbothered by tomorrow's hard work
踊りな踊り念仏、気も軽々と、明日の稼業、苦にならぬ

Good news. I am the beast of my dreams. A cis-man without flag or mountain. Readable, but the sum of extra parts. A pride of claws. What snaggle-toothed king can outpace me among the honeysuckles? The emergency of me, unmanned and lovely.

The village, the village Obon, we can never forget the red face of Enma, Lord of Death
村よの村の御盆よ、御閻魔様の、赤い御顔が、忘すらりよか

RITUAL AGAINST TOXIC MASCULINITY

[00:07]   Entitled as I am to sugar and overflowing milk,
                    I am also a collector of distress.

[00:13]   Even on paper my phylum is overrated.

[00:36]   Did I arrive here singing or insinuating?

[00:58]   Everyone burns, so this is not a condemnation of labor.

[01:04]   By bending into a barb, I learned to man.

[01:22]   In order to violate a blueprint...

[01:23]   Conspire to speed fatal mitosis.

[01:44]   *Water, muscle, berry, shell bone.*

[01:50]   While the filial vessel sleeps, I shake fifty men
                    until they secrete a sweet keening.

[02:09]   We rub antennae and soak, ready for release—

            on the right bodies, holy water will burn.

AS THE LIGHT DIMINISHES AGAIN

To fit the average, we come
as animals, with a pocket map
of the sky and nothing under.[1]

How the ragged hairpiece gapes
open and declares teeth. Again,
godzilla damage and its mathematics
of blister.[2]

We send them back to the cave, but
they fly the fence buried in birds. Once,
I stopped them at the border of my mother. Never
swore anything to any official.[3]

---

1. This is a horizontal clutch called home. A whipped feather, strange marks cleaving our nation of night. We wave bright limbs of alarm. And yet our state, so enchanting.

2. "We act and walk and speak and talk in ways that consolidate an impression of being a man or being a woman."

3. We dusky porters, together in an ark of wet clouds. How slowly we move, with such creature interest. A fieldworker specialized of species.

The republic is a skitter, a skim. Never
met a state worth paying for.[4]

All definitions a membrane of thin.
What holds me up is surface tension.[5]
My shadow walks me to the tower. Says,
sever its steel neck with your pink glitter puff.[6]

Come at me, tyrannosaurus. I'll fill my tank
with you. I'm a map of a man,[7]

I must transmute.
I must be flammable gold.

---

4. Squeeze the blood of our fascination.

5. The sad-voiced bird who can translate a forefinger into a rich display unmatched.

6. 「ギヤテイギヤテイハラギャテイハラソギャテイボジソワカ」
   "gyatei gyatei hara gyatei harasogyatei boji sowaka"

7. Above all marvelous desert, we night-flying ships. We speak precisely through the night. Huge
   birds of endless miles, we burn alone.

THE MONSTROSITY: NOTES TOWARDS A FRANKENPO

I.

Growing up immersed in Japanese intransitive verbs, I learn to omit the subject in a sentence. Later as an adult and a poet, I begin to negate the US American English insistence on explicit subject-verb pairs. Or rather, active negation of the active voice begins. Why should a voice be labeled and gendered as "passive" as if it does nothing? It does much more than it seems: the receiver has to perceive meanings through context. It leaves room for the relationship between the communicators. Or rather, room is left for the meaning to be supplied through relationship.

This is how Godzilla would speak, despite appearances.

II.

His eyes are staring, his mouth is open, his wings are spread. This is how one pictures the angel of history. His face is turned toward the past. Where we perceive a chain of events, he sees one single catastrophe which keeps piling wreckage upon wreckage and hurls it in front of his feet. The angel would like to stay, awaken the dead, and make whole what has been smashed. But a storm is blowing from Paradise; it has got caught in his wings with such violence that the angel can no longer close them. This storm irresistibly propels him into the future to which his back is turned, while the pile of debris before him grows skyward. This storm is what we call progress.

Walter Benjamin on Paul Klee's monoprint, *Angelus Novus*, in "Theses on the Philosophy of History" (1942).

Paul Klee's *Angelus Novus* is a rogue taxidermy, an anatomically reversed griffin. A wild mane whips around the lion-like face, uneven teeth frame an expression of surprise, eyes slightly askew. The angel's wings are also hands, recalling a feathered, avian dinosaur, and bird-like legs dangle under a set of tail feathers. This is a "new angel," which for Walter Benjamin, living with and between two world wars, comes to represent the emptiness and horror present in the discursive and material realities of modernity. A witness to the wreckage of modernity, the angel is itself patched together from different beasts. A monstrous presence is needed to respond to monstrous times.

We see this reflected in different poets: Don Mee Choi, Bhanu Kapil, Barbara Jane Reyes, Joyelle McSweeney, Kim Hyesoon, Hōrmi It, Raúl Zurita, and Dolores Dorantes. These are the writers whose work I am most familiar with. Because of centuries of capitalist extremism—colonialism, imperialism, and neoliberalism—damning evidence has piled up. The logic of Progress, the pernicious idea that all of humanity and history always advances towards better conditions under Western guidance, is no logic at all. It is a dissipating magic spell. It has failed because its pretense of universality is just a pretense. The Universal only benefits a few. With right-wing nationalist and neofascist populists sweeping to power in the US and Europe exploiting the cracks in neoliberal capitalism, the wreckage is more evident to both the left and right. It is our response that differs, our political commitment to and solidarity with the historic margins.

III.

I am no doubt not the only one who writes in order to have no face. Do not ask who I am and do not ask me to remain the same: leave it to our bureaucrats and our police to see that our papers are in order. At least spare us their morality when we write.
Michel Foucault, *The Archaeology of Knowledge*

Reading Foucault, I cultivate a suspicion of the master narrative and the all-knowing author in its many forms. For the arrogance of the one who Knows, for the expert whose expertise is universal and marginalizes any alternatives. For the white male explorer whose perspective is unquestionable, unassailable because supposedly neutral, objective, and universal. In response, drawing on Japanese grammar, I experiment with minimizing the Western, hyper-individuated, confessional self—not to efface the hand that writes, but to contextualize it in all that produces it as a cultural point of view. The subject is not solid, but a construction—of history, race, class, gender, religion, and more.

IV.

There are compatible concepts in Buddhism. For instance, practicing Vipassana meditation for many years and experiencing direct glimpses of the changing, contingent nature of self. In the Satipatthana Sutta, there are instructions for a meditation on the body in its physical details, on its organs, fluids, systems, and fibers, each part isolated and reflected on separately. By contemplating each part, equanimity is cultivated and attachment to the body as me or mine is weakened. Through active practice, it becomes possible to loosen the grip on conventional identity, to regard it as a temporary vessel. And yet the conventional self is constantly produced through interaction with its environment. In socially engaged Buddhism, the significance of self, community, and identity is not minimized, because they influence and are influenced by our economic, cultural, and political experiences. There are also ethical precepts, guidelines for cultivating the conditions for happiness and ending suffering, which focuses the gaze back into the world. Holding one's communities and commitments in a field of compassion, a gentle titration ensues between self and un- or re-making the self. This is a poetic practice of self that embraces more than one simultaneous reality, but never ignores the world.

V.

The angelic, floating white woman in John Gast's 1872 painting *American Progress* is a celebration of the colonization of North America, and she is also a monster. An eroticized symbol of an expansionist, selectively benevolent state, beneath the exterior she is Frankenstein's monstrosity, patched together from genocide, slavery, capitalist exploitation, and racialized, gendered violence, blown westward by the force of their explosions. The rest of us, the majority, are either not in this painting or pushed to its edges, buried under its pastoral. Yet in the wreckage we find ways to recycle, compost, to be a worm in the gut of the state. We awaken the dead. Benjamin's angel cannot see the future with its back turned to it, but we create from what is in front of us, and that is a kind of future. It exists not in order to produce use-value, but to create beauty, an effort to resist monetization.

VI.

Gazing back at the wreckage as I am swept towards the future, my family strides onto the path. My grandmother's Japan was/is an imperial power. Buddhism as a tool of domination. By letting go of self in service of a "compassionate" war, the monk-soldier becomes a single-minded, efficient killer. Ideology: to expand the Japanese Empire in order to prevent Europe from conquering Asia. There is the Japanese occupation of my grandfather's Taiwan, 1895-1945. Atomic obliteration in the Pacific, in Japan. The awakening of Godzilla. This too is wreckage, with its long half-life.

VII.

And then, how does one reckon with Confucianism? I consult the online I Ching divination system, digital representative of ancient Chinese heteropatriarchy, rectifier of proper, harmonious social relations. Interviewing the online I Ching (which is itself a British translation), asking it questions it can never really answer that, in a way, are against its own best interest. Dear I Ching, what is the best way to end patriarchy? What is the best way to end white supremacy? Divine your own destruction. Inserting its answers into Google Translate, going through the languages of my family—from English to Traditional Chinese to Japanese and back to English—imitating migration. If Hakka was available this would be included, too. The I Ching's voice is forced to mutate, receding in some places, exploding in others. The imperfection of translation, the impossibility of one-to-one correspondence of meaning, results in the intentional production of wreckage. Like an n+7 Tower of Babel. Cutting up the results, hunting among the trash for useful pieces with which to build new, imperfect responses.

VIII.

I was going to create a new kind of man. This man would love me more than a
son loves his father. I also thought that if I could make lifeless parts live, maybe I
could bring the dead back to life.
    Mary Shelley, *Frankenstein* (abridged)

To choose and collect bodies, to dissect, disaggregate, and randomize parts. To
rearrange and merge, to erase the extraneous, to sew together. To reanimate. For
Dr. Frankenstein, this work begins as a kind of progress, an invention of science
with tremendous potential for human benefit. It ends in tragedy, and a monster
is left to roam the world. Since the European Enlightenment, the language of
universal "progress" has justified colonial and imperial violences both overt
and subtle. It is both "manifest destiny" and the "white man's burden" to spread
North American and European disasters everywhere. Aimé Césaire notes
in *Discourse on Colonialism* that colonial Europe, whose ostensible reason for
being is benevolence while its actual motive is exploitation, is "indefensible."
It has left a trail of lifeless parts in the name of the father. But we can also find
creativity in the middle of trash: we find new relationships between the parts.

    Mutations, reanimations of texts. Digging up bodies, text bodies
with antagonistic relations, mutually generative relations, or seemingly no
relationship at all. Isolating every word, randomizing order, mixing. Using text
manipulation software, moving body parts, organs, systems, from one location
to another. Chopping, erasing, sewing. Searching for new connections, unseen
formations. Building new bodies because the old ones are indefensible. Or
composting—bodies growing out of the indefensibility of the old.

    Not an attempt to create a new kind of man, but to grow a monster
of compassion and ferocity. Because capitalism, white supremacy,
heteropatriarchy is so monstrous, perhaps only a Godzilla can counter it.
Systems of dehumanization proliferate, isolate, and pathologize communities
that deviate from the norm. In solidarity with Godzilla—child of the atomic
bomb—we can commit rogue taxidermy against its texts—a Frankenstein
poetry, a frankenpo. Perhaps only monsters can reinvent humanity, though not
with a replacement humanism or dominant universal. Instead, something only
monsters, having experienced destruction, can imagine—an ethics of mutual

grieving, radical generosity, hospitality. A feral, generous poetry arriving from the future we are always being blown into.

IX.

Isolate the 45th US President's inauguration speech, noted by the *Washington Post* for being uniquely apocalyptic in the history of such speeches. Then dig up the speech given by Senator Palpatine to the Galactic Senate in *Star Wars III: Revenge of the Sith*, in which Palpatine revokes democracy and becomes the Emperor. Isolate words, mixing and randomizing. Search for unique juxtapositions, odd phrases and images. See what connections and contradictions emerge or get amplified.

Find a feminist article discussing the US mainstream emasculation of Asian American men. Mix it with the complete English subtitles from Wong Kar-Wai's sexy Hong Kong masterpiece, *In the Mood for Love*. Or mix an article on Japanese "genderless danshi" with a Buddhist sutta on loving-kindness, and the screenplay of the animated film, *The Last Unicorn*. Through this process, affirm multiple sexualities and gender expressions.

Steal text from an 1845 article in which the phrase "manifest destiny" is first used, justifying the annexation of Texas from Mexico. Mix it with itself. Fuck it up. What hidden messages emerge? How can the text be used to implicate itself?

What indefensible monstrosities do we come from, live in? What new bodies do we need in order to survive and live? What texts can we conjure from the wreck, whose ferocious griffin hospitality can we inhabit? Can we awaken the dead?

X.

A monstrous poetry,[1] troubling the text. The world as text. Kaiju/Godzilla poetry. Mutant poetry. Cyborg poetry.[2] Feral,[3] necropastoral[4] poetry. Undocumented poetry. Taxidermy poetry.[5] Witch/brujx poetry.[6] Cunt-up poetry.[7] Compost poetry. Literary rasquachismo.[8] A trash aesthetic.[9] Poetry with little use for the shiny, never-quite-fulfilled or fulfilling promises of modernity, nationalisms, neoliberalism. Cross-translating between worlds, between English and Englishes, between the past, now, and what might come. Not translating for clarity or legibility, but to point out gaps and the power relations that create them.[10] Composting the master narrative and growing new bodies, new abilities. Diving into the wreckage.[11] We need poetry that already knew it was political, and didn't have to be convinced.

What is the subject being produced through frankenpo? One who makes and remakes, exactly because destruction has never been complete. There are always parts leftover. Though intersectional and inseparable from the wreck, we also become ferociously different—imperfect, wild, succulent. A monstrously generous poetry, in a world of inhuman monstrosity.

---

1. Sor Juana Inés de la Cruz
2. Margaret Rhee
3. Bhanu Kapil
4. Joyelle McSweeney
5. Rajiv Mohabir
6. Angel Dominguez
7. Dodie Bellamy
8. Amalia Mesa-Bains and Tomás Ybarra-Frausto
9. Ben Highmore
10. Jen Hofer
11. Adrienne Rich

91

With thanks to Vickie Vértiz and Heidi Andrea Restrepo Rhodes for their generative readings and interventions. There are many more poets whose work could be noted here.

NOTES

"Visa" is a frankenpo combining texts of Presidential Executive Orders 13769 and 13780 (Protecting the Nation from Foreign Terrorist Entry into the United States) + Octavia Butler's The Books of the Living, verses 1-66 + Reflection on the Repulsiveness of the Body from the Satipatthana Sutta.

"Portrait of grandfather as a cowboy" contains furigana over certain words and phrases. In conventional use, furigana is a Japanese reading aid that indicates pronunciation, though here it is used either to clarify meaning or to create double meaning.

"Teaching men to be emotionally honest" is a frankenpo of the April 9, 2016 New York Times article "Teaching Men to Be Emotionally Honest" + www.askmen. com article "Traits Of A Real Man: Welcome To The Only Handbook You'll Ever Need To Becoming A Real Man." Quotes from New Order (2), Sei Shonagon (5), Adrienne Rich (6), Fred Moten (9), Dolores Dorantes (12), and the Metta Sutta (13).

"Footnotes to a murder in the third degree" is a frankenpo of the August 9, 2017 New York Times Magazine article "What a Fraternity Hazing Death Revealed About the Painful Search for an Asian-American Identity" by Jay Caspian Kang + the screenplay of Nagisa Oshima's 1999 film Gohatto (御法度) + Mutsuo Takahashi's erotic story "The Hunter." Quotes from Wikipedia entry on football (3), Confucius (7), The New York Times Magazine, August 9, 2017 (9, 14, 17), Theresa Hak Kyung Cha (12), Eve K. Sedgwick (16), and New Order (18).

"She's people! 10 apologies" is a frankenpo combining celebrity sexual misconduct apologies from Ben Affleck, Matt Lauer, Russell Simmons, Roy Moore, Charlie Rose, James Toback, George H.W. Bush, Harvey Weinstein, Louis C.K., Kevin Spacey, George Takei, and Aziz Ansari.

"Dear I Ching, am I a real man?" is a poem constructed using the results of a consultation with an online I Ching divination website.

"Stomach me, delicious world" is a frankenpo combining the screenplay of Wong Kar-Wai's *Happy Together* (1997) + the screenplay of Alice Wu's *Saving Face* (2004) + the July 13, 2015 article, "Confucius on Gay Marriage," in *The Diplomat* + the August 25, 2005 *New York Times* article "Court in Hong Kong Invalidates Antisodomy Law from British Era."

"Maggie and Tony" is a frankenpo of the screenplay of Wong Kar-Wai's *In the Mood for Love* (2000) + the October 20, 2015 *Everyday Feminism* article "5 Reasons Why We Need to Change the Way We Talk About 'Emasculating' Asian Men."

"Dear I Ching, what is the legacy of colonization in my family?" is a poem constructed using the results of a consultation with an online I Ching divination website and translated excerpts from the diary of my paternal great-grandmother, Jiang San-Mei.

"Notorious rain" is a frankenpo combining Japanese and translated English dialogue from Akira Kurosawa's *Rashomon* (1950) + US presidential Executive Order 9066 (1942).

"I bite with inaccurate teeth" is a frankenpo of a speech by POTUS45 + a white supremacist manifesto by DSR + a reflection on the repulsiveness of the body (Patikkulamanasikara) in the Satipatthana Sutta + the essay by Grace Lee Boggs, "Naming the Enemy."

"Manifest destiny for sassy choir" is a frankenpo of John L. O'Sullivan's "The Great Nation of Futurity" (1839), first known instance of the phrase "manifest destiny" + a found transcription of "The Star Spangled Banner" as played by Jimi Hendrix at Woodstock (1969).

"Now I know what it's like" is a frankenpo of the essay "Hypermasculinity and Violence as a Social System" by Thomas J. Scheff + chapter 10 of *Frankenstein* by Mary Shelley (1986 abridged version).

"Dear I Ching, how does hetero-patriarchy live on through me?" is a poem constructed using the results of a consultation with an online I Ching divination website. Uses multiple masculine Japanese versions of "you" descending in politeness, starting with very formal and ending with extremely rude.

"Wanted bodies become animals" is a frankenpo of news articles on cowboy theme parks, a men's rights opinion piece, "10 Reasons To Own An AR-15" + Chapter 4 of *Frankenstein* by Mary Shelley (1986 abridged version). Varying typefaces indicate different sources for specific words.

"Empire strikes" is a frankenpo of Emperor Palpatine's speech to the Galactic Senate (*Star Wars* Ep 3 - Revenge of the Sith) + POTUS 45's inaugural speech + selected dialogue involving the Emperor from *Star Wars* Ep 4-6.

"Drowsiness through my kiss" is a frankenpo of an article on genderless danshi + the Metta Sutta (Karaniyametta Sutta) + the screenplay of the animated movie *The Last Unicorn* (1982).

"Descending, throttle early, savagely" is a frankenpo of the screenplay of *Purple Rain* (1984).

"Letter to Chow Mo-wan" is a frankenpo of the screenplay for Wong Kar-Wai's *In the Mood for Love* + the violin part of Shigeru Umebayashi's "Yumeji's Theme" + Tony Leung Chiu-wai's *Greatest Hits* (梁朝偉精選) + quotes from Eve K. Sedgwick. Uses "feminine" gendered Japanese sentence endings.

"My boy band throws national shade" contains a line spoken by the replicant Roy Batty in the film *Blade Runner* (1982).

"The goat man cancels his enemies" is a frankenpo of lines from *The Mask of Fu Manchu* (1932) + *Charlie Chan at the Opera* (1936) + Chinese Exclusion Act (1882) + Mettanisamsa Sutta + Patisambhidamagga Sutta.

"Self-portrait as Voltron" is accompanied by the lyrics and transcription of a bon odori song that originated in the Japanese American community, simply titled "Bon Odori Uta" (盆踊り歌).

"Ritual against toxic masculinity" is a frankenpo of the screenplay of Justin Lin's *Better Luck Tomorrow* (2002) + Confucian Analects 1.1 (475 BC–221 BC) + Chinese Exclusion Act (1882).

"As the light diminishes again" contains quotes from Judith Butler (2) and the Heart Sutra (般若心経) (6).

RECENT TITLES FROM ALICE JAMES BOOKS

Soft Science, Franny Choi
Bicycle in a Ransacked City: An Elegy, Andrés Cerpa
Anaphora, Kevin Goodan
Ghost, like a Place, Iain Haley Pollock
Isako Isako, Mia Ayumi Malhotra
Of Marriage, Nicole Cooley
The English Boat, Donald Revell
We, the Almighty Fires, Anna Rose Welch
DiVida, Monica A. Hand
pray me stay eager, Ellen Doré Watson
Some Say the Lark, Jennifer Chang
Calling a Wolf a Wolf, Kaveh Akbar
We're On: A June Jordan Reader, Edited by Christoph Keller and Jan Heller Levi
Daylily Called It a Dangerous Moment, Alessandra Lynch
Surgical Wing, Kristin Robertson
The Blessing of Dark Water, Elizabeth Lyons
Reaper, Jill McDonough
Madwoman, Shara McCallum
Contradictions in the Design, Matthew Olzmann
House of Water, Matthew Nienow
World of Made and Unmade, Jane Mead
Driving without a License, Janine Joseph
The Big Book of Exit Strategies, Jamaal May
play dead, francine j. harris
Thief in the Interior, Phillip B. Williams
Second Empire, Richie Hofmann
Drought-Adapted Vine, Donald Revell
Refuge/es, Michael Broek
O'Nights, Cecily Parks
Yearling, Lo Kwa Mei-en
Sand Opera, Philip Metres
Devil, Dear, Mary Ann McFadden

Alice James Books is committed to publishing books that matter. The press was founded in 1973 in Boston, Massachusetts as a cooperative, wherein authors performed the day-to-day undertakings of the press. This element remains present today, as authors who publish with the press are invited to collaborate closely in the publication process of their work. AJB remains committed to its founders' original feminist mission, while expanding upon the scope to include all voices and poets who might otherwise go unheard. In keeping with its efforts to build equity and increase inclusivity in publishing and the literary arts, AJB seeks out poets whose writing possesses the range, depth, and ability to cultivate empathy in our world and to dynamically push against silence. The press was named for Alice James, sister to William and Henry, whose extraordinary gift for writing went unrecognized during her lifetime.

Designed by Anna Reich
annareichdesign.com

Printed by McNaughton & Gunn